PARENTING PERCEPTIONS

INSIGHTFUL ESSAYS FOR THE NURTURER

SHOURYA CHOUREY

OF FRAMEWORK

We live and work with a specific framework during various stages of our lives. We choose some contexts, and others are stages of life which each of us goes through. It's important to note here that not everyone has experienced every framework. Sometimes two people might meet in the common area of two or more concentric frames. In such cases, perception and instinct should play a significant role because obviously, we want to live and work in unanimity, don't we?

In India, children get to choose their framework after almost eighteen long years as to what they would like to study further, and obviously, the college provides freedom most of them have not fathomed existed. So here is a question to think about, is it college freedom that's taking the toll on kids? Or is it the before college time that is finally taking its toll; a good question to mull over, but we will get back to this later, for now, let's discuss the framework.

In a newborn child's journey to their teenage years, there is a constant and tumultuous shift of framework for them. It starts with understanding language, then discovering new things and how they operate, then pleasing their parents and relatives, then being with peers and listening to their teachers. Just listing these things out made me feel cumbersome. Paradigm shifts have become a general norm for our society and followed so blindly, we have forgotten their purpose of creation. That one grows up and can work within this world and make their truth is often forgotten. So blindly do we follow these enlisted frameworks that the scope to be ourselves is minimal, and thus this trend of self-discovery has become a huge thing today.

Most children don't get time or aren't intelligent enough at their tender ages to know that knowing about themselves is a big chunk of the pie that makes up a satiating life for themselves. The set standards are not outrightly wrong, but ego drives each one of us. To do the bidding of our egos healthily, we need to find our truths. In the pursuit of this, there should be no labeling. Labeling has become such a vast and latent social evil that it can steer the course of an individual and our society in the direction of doom. In this scenario, when a child is discovering things, it is essential to detach from them at various stages, but labeling something as right or wrong or merely repeating the phrase 'say no to drugs' won't help. Children are much more receptive than rigid adults, so the logic behind everything will provide them with scope for self-development and mental nourishment, and no, it shall not make their childhood any less.

Childhood should now become the pious age of imparting know-ledge to them, whatever their nature may be, even violent or sexual or philosophical. Wouldn't it be better if the parents show the children the world and what to expect rather than the world crashing down on their children? Indeed, we cannot prepare children for everything they will face, and this truth should be the strength of today's parents.

The children are busy adapting to continuous changes in their framework. They are new to this, so if there isn't a smooth transition or closure for them from a previous frame, they will try to recreate that part throughout their lives, thinking that their happiness is lying in that incomplete frame that didn't have a closure or a solid reasoning behind it. And this recreation on their part can become harmful at every level possible. To avoid such situations, the adults in a child's life have to do one thing. They have to know the difference between imparting and imposing. Of course, there will be situations where one would have to practise a gentle form of imposing, but later, the child would understand that it was worthwhile. But looking at the situation today, there is no distinction or differentiation on the adult's part. They think that the children won't understand, and without giving their children proper scope, they start imposing their reality on the child. This is the most toxic thing one could do to a child.

Children being more receptive are prone to adapt to realities they are imposed upon, which would later prove to stunt their mental and emotional growth. Then the child is lacerated with phrases that, at a certain age, they are such and such. To make them build their concrete reality in which they can work, they need to be adaptive and create them, so there have to be many counter-intuitive approaches in their daily life challenges. That is when they will really know and acknowledge the things they are experiencing. Just like reading self-help books without implementing them in one's life won't make anyone wiser, the children will not become wiser only by being stated the rights & wrongs and asking them to listen. A very rare minority of children are capable to do that in a manner which promotes their holistic growth. When they go out of the cocoon, they may never, in actuality, realize and acknowledge those teachings of right & wrong, this would create an endless void in their lives.

Our world is imposing at every level. Even the best of us live lost in our own void, so just imagine the plight of a new life imposed upon since birth. It's imperative here to understand that each child is unique in their own way, and adults are covering that uniqueness under the layers of their imposed reality. Following the rigid unwritten rules of society as a parent has also taken a significant toll on their children. If the children are not allowed to navigate through their possibilities, they will end up not 'misusing' but 'using' that college freedom, and then those things would happen, which would have had to take place much earlier in their lives. Here the label of misuse is used by the adults, whereas in reality the child, according to their stunted understanding, is 'using' the college freedom to explore and navigate through the various possibilities in life

Labeling has become generic, and it is essential to come out of it; every one of us is living in the closet of labeling. To abolish this toxic practice, everyone first needs to go out and acknowledge that we do it every time. There is a thin line of demarcation between labeling and stating things in their proper context. The context is important here. Children need to be taught how perception and meanings work so that they start thinking in the units of knowledge and background, which would increase the scope for their holistic development and reasoning capabilities.

Finally, we all need to know that the world is currently surviving under a clash of personalities and ideologies. Therefore, everyone is trying to find their personal harmony rather than a conscious societal one. Children need to know and acknowledge this clash more than the parent's own reality being imposed on them.

OF DEMARCATIONS

We can all agree that our minds have evolved in such a manner that we can perform the function of demarcation to lead our lives. For when we are children, the demarcation imbibed in by us from our parents and guardians is in the form of dos and donts.

After we step into adulthood, when we understand that we can do things in the donts list, we incline towards achieving the donts. Why? We want to find our own truth, our own meanings to something, we want to discover for ourselves because that would give us a lot of power and depth at the same time. Following what someone says always makes us feel lesser of ourselves sometimes, and when this becomes the situation, we get confused as to our own discoveries, our own identity, and there forms a massive void in us.

This void in us needs to be fed and catered with lots of ice cream before sleeping or lots of ice cream for breakfast. If our parents have not inculcated sufficient fear in us or are more adventurous, we try to fill this void by abusing substances or living life on the wild and unruly side, trying to form our own reality. This go-to is not wrong, for we have always tended towards having the forbidden, especially when it gives us a high. It gives us something we have not experienced before, and so an individual feels that they are closer to the fabric of their reality and thus providing an ego boost at the same time. Could the demarcation here that we won't commit substance abuse have made us a lesser being? Maybe, maybe not. The abuse would have been an experience, and for us, experiences matter the most, as they form the core of our reality through which we operate in our lives. But are we all equipped enough to learn from those experiences? No, not really. Even the most observant of us can't even register the experiences they go through each day, so learning from them is different. This happens because early in our lives, we are taught to learn from our bad experiences only and gradually this enters into our conditioning. It's a very toxic thing, and there is no way around it, it seems. For kids, yes, sure, they need to fall down to learn to walk, but for adults, do they need to go deep in that void or deeper into themselves?

The advent of Social Media has made our society more connected, and therefore, the hunger for what others have has increased. More than anything, every individual has to feed his ego, and so in a society, they need to be in the loop, especially teenagers and young adults. Culture has romanticized things just because someone has become rich or a celebrity in dire situations. We measure success with power, money, education, and fame. So everyone tries to follow or instead mimic them with their success stories. Here comes the function of demarcation.

Here we must see demarcation with clarity. During our lives, however idealistic one becomes, everyone will practice demarcation. Because life is so full of diverse experiences, our demarcations will mostly be temperamental and temporary.

Here, it is highly prudent to say that demarcation is not this line of discipline. Discipline is usually looked down upon by teenagers and young adults. They are not wrong looking down upon it; they just haven't found the things they need to be disciplined for; it's as simple as, 'why would a customer come to a cafe on the behest of its owner's request just because the owner says that at that time the coffee will taste like chocolate'. Still, the customer doesn't care about that; that particular customer wants his coffee to keep him awake so he could work; what the hell does he care if it tastes like chocolate or not.

So, apart from demarcations being temporary and temperamental, they are rudimentary at first and work on the conscious and subconscious level. So, the first task here is to acknowledge one's conscious demarcations so that one can work with them according to their morality or integrity, basically the set of things that makes us feel conscientious or, for that matter, the rules which form one's conscience. Once we have known where our conscious demarcations stand, most of the subconscious ones will be revealed to the individual in a particular passage of time. Knowing these demarcations formed by an individual, the individual will be closer to oneself. Remember, at this time, things will come out which may not adhere to societal standards.

These societal standards could be helpful for an individual or detrimental. They can be beneficial and harmful in two spheres of an individual's life - social and personal. Though one leads a life in society, an individual has a private sphere that significantly shapes their social life and vice versa. The nature of our demarcations caters to both - Social sphere and the personal sphere; if they are working in harmony, it's good, and if not, both the spheres suffer.

It's important to note here that whatever our demarcations may be, we can always improvise to suit ourselves better. One would also do much good to just acknowledge that they commit to the practice of demarcations, and then the process of accepting them should come. One would realize that our standard of life is set by the demarcations we have developed.

Knowing one's own demarcations, an individual comes close to realizing their strengths and weaknesses. But the plus point here is that one can attain more powers, and then one would know that this strength was always there, so here the quest or hunger for one's own discovery gets quenched, and thus we come out of the void we had formed. Sometimes individual feels that the void can be filled with the perspectives generated by substance abuse but what is the need for this harmful add-on when one could discover these things with a little introspection of their demarcations? Imagine how powerful an individual would feel, free to steer the course of their lives in the manner they want.These societal standards could be helpful for an individual or detrimental. They can be beneficial and harmful in two spheres of an individual's life - social and personal. Though he leads a life in society, an individual has a private sphere that significantly shapes his social life and vice versa. The nature of our demarcations caters to both - Social sphere and the personal sphere; if they are working in harmony, it's good, and if not, both the spheres suffer.

It's important to note here that whatever our demarcations may be, we can always improvise to suit ourselves better. One would also do much good to just acknowledge that they commit to the practice of demarcations, and then the process of accepting them should come. One would realize that our standard of life is set by the divisions we have developed.

Knowing one's own demarcations, an individual comes close to realizing their strengths and weakness. But the plus point here is that one can attain more powers, and then one would know that this strength was always there, so here the quest or hunger for one's own discovery gets quenched, and thus we come out of the void we had naturally. Substance abuse might get one. There might not; this process will be the same, so why take the extra measure of committing to a substance. Wouldn't it be a wonderful feeling to discover these things on your own? Imagine how powerful an individual would feel, free to steer the course of one's life in the manner one wants.

OF LABELLING

The world was never as connected as it is today; electricity, cell-phones, televisions, the internet. This is the age of social media.

In this interconnected age where people are more in touch online than in real life, the world scenario has changed, and this acts as the most significant catalyst in labeling. Labeling has risen to such an extent throughout the world that it can be called one of the most potent social evil existing today.

Labeling in our society illuminates the shortcomings of our community, which are -

-Being lazy

-Lack of empathy

-Lack of value of life

-Spiteful

-Superficial and Hypocrite

This list is not exhaustive but made to gather the essence of what is wrong with us as individuals and a society.

This generalization of a group or individual limits the scope of one who labels and is labeled. This can stunt our growth as an individual and a society. This hampers us to tap into the potential of an individual or group thereby, limiting and exhausting resources that could have been a boon to societal development. Of course, Children who are highly receptive are majorly affected by labeling. It has become such rampant that labeling has become an unwritten norm of our society.

Such limited has become the scope of our parenting and initial education that children, teenagers, adolescents, and scarily even adults are sucked into the vicious cycle of labelling and remain there. One could only imagine the plight of one's country where the young population blithely and unknowingly practices labelling. Soon the process enters the same neurons of the receptive young brain, and it becomes a very deeply inculcated habit that will most probably never end, and in most cases, the wrong in it won't even be realized. Such intricate is the web labeling has formed over our society.

Some of us have a basic understanding of how our psyche works, and some of us don't know; both are reasons good enough to realize the ill effects labelling could cause.

Generalization, however, is not wrong always, as sometimes it shows us our reflection and what is wrong with us, but only a minuscule number of it is used in such a manner. Some people can overcome even the most rigorous labelling as they know their potential or simply don't care. But not everyone is equally strong-minded; for a harmonious co-existence in today's developed and developing world, we need to find the major and minor fault lines in us, and the society to fill them with understanding.

A person is so much more than just one thing. It's a heart-wrenching thing that needs to be mentioned in this era of intellectual growth. Of course, we can process only so much in our lifetimes. We can only connect with a limited number of people. So it becomes necessary to compartmentalize our lives, but doing so by practicing the toxicity of labelling is self-deprecating also. Already, there are so many problems of mere survival that an individual goes into a cocoon which becomes very difficult to break without proper help, for intellect has its darker side like everything else. And labeling generates a void which limits the possibilities in a life of both, the labelled and the one who labels.

'Dangerously Ubiquitous' is the term to describe today's labelling era; after all, it has become an innocuous-looking norm of the society. Such intricately has it woven its web in our community that if labelling is openly discussed for its perils, we will discover that it has become intricately indispensable to our society. There will be utter chaos as each one has labelled others and even themselves. Further, it has infested itself in the pillars of our democracy and politics. The change must come from within ourselves by realizing and acknowledging the havoc it creates in at various stage of our lives.

Labeling is gross misconduct, especially in today's age where one is latently bombarded by a plethora of things through the media, there is a reality that is sold, and we buy it, clouding our integral rationale reality. No one today has an individual mindset; we all try to, but such is the bombardment of needless things that we fail to build a sound and healthy perspective of ourselves and the world we live in. Labeling adds to this chaotic cluster making one intoxicated in the worst possible manner. A labyrinth unbeknownst to us has been created in us, and we become lost in it, and even new experiences have stopped jolting us down to come out of this labyrinthine cocoon, failing to realize our true potential, our true selves. What could be more toxic for a society which misuses its power of creating demarcations in such a disorderly manner?

OF COMMUNICATION

At an early age, children are highly receptive and curious. They look around them and try to mimic, to be a part of their surrounding activities. If one understands this thing, then it will be followed up by another deeper realization that there is a lot of scope for developing a child, but it is also limited at a certain age. We know things in our inner conscience; in a child, it has to be developed. Also, they are infinitely flexible but also rigid in a manner they can't control; they have no idea of the 'grey' areas. At their tender ages, things are just good or bad for them, and due to their innocent minds' curious and receptive nature, they could even change the good stuff for them into bad things. For example, eating an ice-cream brick in one sitting and then complaining of stomach cramps. Of course, most parents realize these things as they care for their babies but are not used to such intensive care. As soon as the child begins to walk, most of us get relieved that now they can have some free time. The truth is that as a baby, the care was more of a physical one, and as the child grows, we think enough has been done and forget the latent emotional factor.

It is of imminent importance to know here that there should also be the birth of a nurturer in us with the birth of a child. Yes, we get to be mother nature to our children. We are the ones to nurture and nourish them. As soon as a child steps in the communication regime, there should be a conducive environment, at least at home. As mentioned earlier, the child will first try to mimic the words, the body language, the tone, and sooner than one would realize, it will form as a habit and then a way of expressing themselves.

Whether the children realize it or not, patronizing tones should be totally abolished. They are toxic for the emotional growth of their brains. We should talk to them as individuals. And, No! by practising talking to them as individuals we won't be destroying their 'innocent' childhood; instead, we would be enhancing the whole experience. They will be able to express themselves confidently. Extreme emotions of happiness and disappointment are natural when we put so much of ourselves into our children. We must control them, and find a conducive way to vent. We have decided to bring them into the world; we should always communicate with them tin a manner where children feel that they are wanted.

One should understand that what a parent is trying to impart or teach might confuse them during their mistakes. Children don't yet know that we still don't know things after all the knowledge we have acquired; one should embrace this thing, humble their egos, and put it on a tight leash. This would also prove hugely beneficial for the nurturer's self-development. One thing that could help with this is constantly acknowledging that there is an image of perfect we have formed, which is also flawed in ways we don't know. So the children should be given a wider scope to be themselves so that they can form their own self-image and reality in a healthy manner. We should let them grow in directions they want to, and if they don't stick in the same direction, then that is not a flaw or a problem with the child. It's simply a process they undertake unbeknownst to most of them to understand what they are surrounded with, they are trying to fathom a positive possibility in this imperfect world.

In this imperfect world, if we see our child doing something not worthy in our eyes, then we don't need to reprimand them in an angry or subversive manner. Simply put, there is no need to nitpick after the child's process of adapting and evolving, even it has some flaws. Of course, these flaws shouldn't be harmful for the child's growth and must be corrected with a positive approach that involves rationale discussions. Children would need to establish a new approach for adapting and evolving at every certain age. Help your children recognize these stages and help them achieve making such processes. These things obviously, cannot be discussed theoretically as written here as they require practice; through practice, these things can be tailor-made for each child's unique needs.

At a certain time of realisation there will be a gnawing need to re-discover oneself when we notice that we are having a terrible influence on our child in one way or the other. Obviously, no one is perfect, but we can at this point change for the child's and our own betterment. The adults can come face to face with their egos if they are true nurturers of their children, and that is the first and last bell to change and make their child, at least from their perspective, better than them.

OF THE POWER

It is becoming increasingly challenging to survive today, especially with the number of essential things increasing exponentially: thus, prioritizing has become necessary.

There are a plethora of important things in each of our lives. Such is the dynamic nature of survival today that we have to prioritize one crucial thing from another, but there are things in our lives that never fare in our list of essential items. One of those crucial things is a gift we possess to give to the future generation and ourselves. It's just that there is a process to get this gift, a simple one. But such are the complicated, uncanny, ignorant and, convoluted ways we lead our lives today that we are consciously not only getting away from the gift but hell-bent on destroying it.

Humanity has reached a stage where they recognize the power within but can't control it and thus, misuse it. The misuse happens due to various reasons, and to give an idea of its essence, we become prone to abuse it when we hold that power by dividing it and not as a whole. Because when we use our power as a whole, we know we will come above our ignorant ways. We are now scared of that as we will eventually come to face our egos.

Simply put, we have the power to change our future generations into something better. We all know there is always a scope of improvement in our imperfect and flawed lives. The problem arises when we as parents think that the power is absolute in front of the younger age human beings, Children. This feeling of absolute power blurs the difference between imparting and imposing making our parenting practices toxic for the child's holistic growth. There is only so much we could impose before a mutiny; hasn't humanity learned that by now? Don't we want to make our child question things aloud and in tune with us? What would happen if the child is not given a chance to do that and, in his ignorant and yet developed mind, starts forming his own notions of reality that would prove detrimental to the child's growth?

Sometimes a problem in a particular child was actually started or discovered as a solution by the child to a specific thing he perceived wrongly or innocently. This happened because in processing and dealing with a new reality, he was alone. There is a certain age of a child(different for each child) when they simply cannot be left alone, physically and emotionally. Imagine one of the humans is sent to a distant planet similar to earth. Maybe they have a different way of living; their technology works differently than ours. At that time, whether they are advanced or backward in their technology, what we will experience is a feeling of being lost and curious. We know we are lost because we have experienced it, but the child doesn't know that in a way; he is lost and has to pave his own path. So wouldn't it be simple to at least point out where the course is futile or dangerous? Yes, it is, and we teach them, that would be the standard answer! But what about the paths we have not explored? What about the ways we don't know? Most of us concentrate on the path we regret taking and misuse our power, indirectly hurling the child on the same course, thinking we can now tackle it. Do we know what lies there when we have not trodden on it, or are our experiences enough to perceive what lies on the way and what lies on that path for a particular child?

Of course, this counter-intuitive approach should also be used for parents' themselves and then introduce it to their children. The nurturer's and the child's path will have some familiar sights where they could amicably meet and decide to go ahead. It's in our power to make such standard meeting points, so imposing on a child is regressive. We all know we become careless with the role as the kid starts understanding, but one should look at themselves and recall all those moments when they needed proper guidance, and they didn't get it. Obviously, we won't be able to light every path for the child, but it's in our power to give the children a light for themselves, and children being receptive do have the ability to realize this light they have been given.

We have the power to care and nurture and this in itself is a positive thing. How did we make it into something which could be abused knowingly and unknowingly? The answer to this lies in our own upbringing; no need to find where the first instance was but proper observation will lead to the fact that the notion we get of absolute power corrupts the very fabric of the ability to care, nurture and nourish the child with positive seeds of perspectives that will bloom into something worthy. Most of us feel that the power in itself has changed them and made them superior in a manner, but the truth is it was always within us, but we didn't realize it because our own parents didn't. This is not a war where one country is attacked first, and so the other country retaliates; this is as noble and important as it gets. We get a second chance with our children to grow up properly, in a manner we would have preferred. Due to our ignorant ways, the power to realize this beautiful truth has slipped from our beings. But, not entirely because we grasp it and then lose it; it's a slippery path where we need to support each other. We can choose where this arduous slippery path leads us; imagine the beauty in this process. When used in the manner it was designed to use, this power can keep us and our future generations on a path of harmony, and aren't we all looking for peace, that peace which completes our existence into a wholesome one?

The word, 'Power', might be taken here in some negative light, but it is essential to realize that we are making a stand and warding of the negatives in our existing society. Hence, power denotes something really positive in the context. Instead, in this context of parenting, we can use the words' 'ability' or 'potential' interchangeably, which cannot be misinterpreted by us, thereby lowering the scope of 'absolute power' as discussed above. Since we use the words 'able' or 'potential' as something we have achieved or have inherent in us, these words should be repeated in our minds to lower down the negative connotations of the word. 'Power'.

Being able or having the potential to be a nurturer in totality will provide us with perceptions we have never had before; of course, such perceptions need to be put into action according to the unique needs of the child being nurtured. Simply put, the approach has to be tailor-made for an individual child; we must acknowledge that we can do this. In this context, we must realize that what works for one child may not be for the other, and bringing out these comparisons in front of children will ultimately prove toxic. It's not only about talking with them in a gentle voice, remembering that patronizing doesn't work, and remembering that if one decides to talk, then that is the medium they have chosen to impart knowledge, consciousness, and experiences. Of course, when one is deep in the process, one may encounter various permutations and combinations. Sticking to only one way every time will saturate the child, remember the child is curious and notices every new thing that comes across them. This builds a hunger for interacting and being interacted with in novel manners until they stick to something. We have to acknowledge that there will come a development process when the child adheres to a set of things. When this scenario arises, it is essential to not keep pushing. At this point, one should work with their rigidity and flexibility to self-realize what would be feasible for them when they are in a society. Again, nothing will be perfect or absolute, but this thing has to be realized so that they form two essential habits - Striving and Adapting(in a manner which doesn't create a void in them as to how to express themselves truthfully, they need to stand tall for who they are and who they are striving to be).

We as nurturers can make them understand and develop the potential to know that no values or norms are absolute but still at the same time work as constant and variables interchangeably depending on the situation. Further, the child must be nurtured in a manner that generates an acknowledgment that, 'one cannot fathom every problem in one's life, but it is prudent to make one's own perception about it and go about it logically'.

Finally, we must use our ability to nurture a child in a manner that provides an individual processing psyche that readily realizes & acknowledge things they will come across in their lives because, without such a mechanism, the child will always remain lost.Finally, we must use our ability to nurture a child in a manner that provides an individual processing psyche that readily realizes & acknowledge things they will come across in their lives because, without such a mechanism, the child will always remain lost.

OF SUPERFICIALITY

Our lives have turned into a variety of complex facades. There was a time when we lived to hunt, eat and survive. Our development as a species has converted the survival definition, at least for most of us. Convenience and accessibility have played a massive role in changing the meaning of survival. It has transformed into a race where our destination is the finish line. The importance of the journey and cherishing those moments come to only a few of us. Some have achieved what they wanted to and are satisfied with it. They have even changed their definition of achievements and taken a more pragmatic and holistic approach to the reality of their lives. Obviously, these people who can do this are minuscule, and most of this tiny portion is a little too late to get there.

Each individual now has to start their journey with the already circulating ideologies; without realizing this fact, they soon become trapped and claustrophobic in their own minds. Most of us don't get to acknowledge that we have our own minds and a system that could lead to an inner awakening that could diminish the effects of the various superficial propaganda engulfing the world. There are stages in our lives where we need some guidance, a direction, but we have gone numb to these things as unbeknownst to us, we all have involuntary joined the race, a race to above all fit in. Why this desperation for fitting in? It is because of our superficial approach.

We obviously don't realize when the superficial approach comes to us. When we are at a very receptive age, we are constantly bombarded with toxic ideologies by the people who don't even know that they are actually 'imposing' an 'ideology' which can hamper our holistic growth. This thing is still deep into the darker abyss of our mind as it has been going on for generations, and each generation tweaks it according to their convenience, making the hurdle more convoluted and heinous.

The fact that our lives are measured at every level possible to meet 'certain set standards' one showcases the direction we are going. This measurement denotes control. Isn't it a superficial approach to control things? Doesn't it seem that we are going towards seemingly achieving 'absolute power'? The moment we think we are in control, we lose it, and this is the truth; we know this deep inside. The problem arises when we try to control that which needs no controlling, we control just for the sake of it; just like a kid who is made to sit on the driver's seat of a vehicle so that he could steer the wheel thinking he is controlling the car.

There is a vast difference between doing things deftly and daftly. Most youths don't know how to realize something and acknowledge it without being hurt in some way or the other, and when this happens, one starts looking at that incident as absolute. Their growth occurs rigidly, just like we have started growing and cutting plants so that they take a particular shape. If our constitution started to define our way of life, then touching other lives and making a positive difference would be a far-fetched dream as we won't be in the fabric of our own lives' experiences.

We can end this nightmare of living superficially only by constantly valuing each and everything. The process of valuing may start mechanically just by repeating its value in our minds, but even this small step can bring a more significant change in our perceptions about knowing life. Then humanity won't have to undergo a crisis to understand a thing's actual value.

If we focus on value, we won't need to preach or give sermons or take out parades to let people know about the importance of our lives; we shall then reach the depths of realization that we are all one root of a big tree of life. We won't need to change the more minor things as this change will come from within without being on the negative side of the beauty of our lives. The change we would see would be automatic, with an inner understanding of ourselves bringing constant tides of inner peace.

The only problem we will face when we start to value is a lack of consciousness. It's not because it's difficult, but the world has developed in a regressive manner at many levels, making us change our use of consciousness during which we don't realize when we are conscious and when we are not. It's a glitch that we can solve by constantly trying to be with our stream of consciousness and sometimes with proper discussion with a group of people trying to go in the same positively conscious direction. The group discussions will make us acknowledge all the problems each one of us has as an individual, making us, in turn, realize that we are all one. But we would need to practice acceptance and humility along with being bluntly honest about our problems. Using the word blunt with honesty is important here as we as species have made a new connotation of 'being honest' as 'being diplomatic.' We practiced this with whom we met, and soon, it became an internal process too. While we call people who hurt or diverge from our set of ideologies blunt and rude, so latently in our society, blunt has become the slang for honesty and in many ways better than the connotations attached to 'being honest.'

OF FRIENDSHIPS

It's a common notion that we should treat our child as a friend, and we should promote this friendship by being frank so that the communication from both the sides doesn't suffer. This would enable an entirely new understanding of our child.

This notion is very close to the truth. In fact, if we genuinely believe in this, we could even make our children know about true nature of friendship. Of course, everyone has their own definition, but we would be able to merge the thin lines between the positive purposes of friendship.

A culture of friendship between parents and their children will require a lot of frankness, and it will have its own set of problems. Still, once this rickety boat is made up, it can easily be converted into the best cruise ship of life, which would be able to avoid the icebergs in not only the child's life but even the parent's life.

The most important point to note in this journey of friendship is to realize that whatever happens, the parent must always be aware that the child is new to this world and yet to develop their own individual thought processes. So until a child is in imminent and immediate harm to themselves or others, a liberal counter-intuitive approach has to be taken without patronizing the parent's parts.

Also, when the child seems to become frank or purely blunt about his thoughts in front of the parent, there must be an approach of listening and identifying the child's inner voice as to what the child is adept at doing or in what things he has shown fluency. If this is done, only then could one successfully steer the child's thoughts into moving ahead and thinking about other perspectives. This will enhance a child's growth, and soon the child would be positively surprising and making their parents speechless with intellectual questions and the parent would fumble searching for the correct answer to their inquisitiveness.

Even if the parent doesn't know how to tackle this sudden profound inquisitiveness of their children, they must answer them in a manner as if they are answering an adult, enabling them to see the 'grey' areas. A proper tackle of this new-found inquisitiveness would make the child emotionally intelligent, worldly, and even spiritually stronger, and most importantly, this approach will also enable a constructive built of their conscience.

There will be occasions when the parent might feel that there is no point in explaining to their kids, or there is no point in repeating the explanation as the last time the child didn't get it. But this inquisitiveness needs to be tended to in a rigorous manner. This approach to tackle the child's inquisitiveness will be beneficial for the child's future too.

Children connect with their peers because they find a common point in them or wonder about the same things? Sometimes such common grounds have depth in them, so the friendship lasts longer, and sometimes, as children are prone to, the common ground is just for fun, and the friendship doesn't last that long.

Parents must balance between depth and plain fun with their growing child so that their dependency on their friends is a bare minimum. Gradually, as the child grows up, we must consciously tread them on a path of self-discovery. But putting them there, they must not feel they are being left alone. Remember, just like a child's cycle is held by their parent, and after some time, they realize how they have been cycling without their support for quite some time, and they gain confidence in those moments and start to cycle alone. This process is critical and must seem to be very innocuous, or the child can develop anxiety and feel themselves to be incompetent if they don't fare well.

As friendly parents, our job will be to have regular talks like we had with our friends; we should not consider anything less critical, even if that is the case in the long term. Just because a parent might have grown out of some minor things they held importantly doesn't mean the same thing will be minor for their children too, they might need help to steer their way through those same things the parent found easy to surf upon during their childhood. Remember, every child is unique in their own way.

There must be awareness of the child's consciousness. We must remember how we felt during our childhood and understand the child's plight. We must know that the child has strong feelings, and we must go along with their emotions in a healthy manner and try to show the child that such and such things don't really matter with an approach that when the child realizes, they don't feel stupid or insecure about it. This can be achieved by making the child think that what he is experiencing was clearly understood by the parent, and they know how it felt at that time.

Parents often have a notion about being friends with their child, and they just feel that talking to them in a friendly manner is all there is to it, and when they want to say no to something, they show their strictness by affirming themselves to be in power.

To counter this, the parents must give in to the actual reasonable demands of the kid. If the parent doesn't feel up to something, like going for the latest movie, then the parent should indulge them with the truth that they are not in a mood to, rather than just saying no without an explanation or citing a mistake that the child needs to correct before they get their reward. This would make the child realize that parents don't say no to everything and have a life of their own. This will prevent the child from a seemingly unreasonable rebellion, which would cause unnecessary hurdles in their lives. Also, the child won't be caught in the vicious cycle of immediate work and reward system which would diminish the drive of the child in future. Further, the kid will become mature as he is being treated as a true partner in crime with their parent when they decide to go against their set rules and indulge their child in something wrong, but the child wants to experience it for a long time.

For starters, it could be a late-night movie, ice cream for breakfast, or even having that puff from the cigarette the parent often smokes. For now, it's essential that the child knows and has his own naughty experiences just like he would have had with his friend. We all know how dangerous such friendly escapades can become just because there is no thrill in your child's life. Why make the child long for joy when it could be given with a parent's own safety net?

The child will achieve what he wants with these parenting friendships, for a child needs to know that just like their parents and other adults even they are capable to consume knowledge. There is smoother imparting of expertise through friendship rather than a blunt 'No' from their parents without any logical reasoning or explanation.

Obviously, just like our children don't make 'best friends' with their entire class during school, the friendship we need to touch with the child should be tailor-made according to the child.

OF INTENTIONS

A child must know how to demarcate in terms of feasibility and develop an intricate conscience where the child can weigh the advantages and disadvantages of their actions. For this, parents need to showcase their true intention without beating around the bush. Children are pretty receptive at their tender ages, so they will tend to grasp something straightforward.

Obviously, the intention of all the parents is on the line where they want to protect, nurture, care and develop their children into independent, self-sufficient individuals. No parent wants their children to suffer. But it is also essential for the parent to know that suffering is inevitable, and their job is to make sure that the child can handle it constructively.

So if the parent is just busy protecting the child from the realities of life, which the child would one day experience, then that will stunt the child's emotional growth and make the suffering worse as the child won't know how to handle it. This simply means that there is a hurdle called over-protection. The parent should understand their child as an individual to be and decide where imminent protection is needed. If the parent starts dictating even the minor spheres of their child's lives, then the child won't distinguish between the more dangerous or harmful things and will end up confused as to what intention the parent has.

Parents often avoid making their child teach the most basic and simplistic things, thinking it will come naturally. But if the child is cared for and nurtured properly, they will have a context and a perspective to work around during a dire situation. The teaching of the simpler things will have definitive benefits later as their base is clear, just like one needs a clear command of basics of mathematics to later pursue graduation or master's degree in the same.

Often, the parents being well-intentioned come across as unfavorable, bossy, dictatorial, and even toxic in their child's perception. The perspective of the child here is not entirely wrong. Parents sometimes get fed up trying to teach their child a particular thing, habit, or manner; this results in loss of temper. It doesn't mean that the parents always shout at or beat their children, but children being receptive can feel negativity in their parent's behavior. It profoundly impacts them; they feel helpless as they want to be loved and understood by their parents and not make them angry. Here, the child starts making an effort, but some things just don't register at a certain age with some children, and no comparisons should be made with other children.

Only the child knows that it's difficult to understand a particular thing, however well-intentioned their parents are. At this stage, the child must be made to understand in various ways possible. Parents must be conscious that most of the things the child is experiencing are new for him, and the child may not be adept at many things from the start. Every child apart from having their unique potential have their own unique limitations also.

Also, once the child starts being reprimanded for every little thing, there is a loss of interest in learning the way of life, and they tend to go on their own desolate and dangerous path. The parent should avoid making them perfect, for the parents themselves are not perfect, so their idea of perfect will just be an imposition and will again stunt the child's growth.

Parents should tread on the path of making their children aware of their mistakes with admonishment only when they start to know the direction in which the child is adept at learning.

The control that a parent exercises on their children should be measured in a manner where the child has his own space, which could be gradually merged with the well-intentioned logic, learnings, and the parent's knowledge.

If a parent simply starts stating things without any reasoning, thinking that their child is not yet ready, then sooner than they thought, the child will be more than prepared to rebel. When this point is reached, it will be difficult to tread to bring the child back, and the child might even be lost for a long time, and this journey will be desolate and harsh for the child. So even when a parent feels tired or disappointed with their child, they should always make it a point to convey things reasonably and logically so that the true intention of the parent is not lost in translation.

Once the child becomes sure that whatever the parent is showcasing them is for the greater good in the long term, the child will start being frank about his daily life problems. This will be a big step, and most of the parents who reach here will be dumbfounded as to how intelligent their child really is. Of course, the child will grow through various phases in their life, so the parents have to keep up. The job might seem tedious at the beginning.

Still, a parent must remember that it was their choice to bring the child into this world, and they will soon get adapted to this role and even find it to be nourishing and eye-opening for themselves, thereby making them happy as they would learn more about themselves and life in general.

This is not the era of pure survival; the child should be given a conducive environment to grow so that they know how downtrodden people really are, both emotionally and financially, but it should stop there. They shouldn't be imposed with negative situations far away from them because that would highly limit their scope of development and improvement. If the child is constantly badgered about the poor condition their parents came from and that the child is so lucky, then they will, unbeknownst to them, start feeling incompetent and undeserving.

This doesn't mean the children's whims should be accepted but make them reason in such a manner as to how they can demarcate between their tender age's need, want, and whims. This demarcation can be enabled by questioning the kid's actions and seeking an answer from them. Still if the child doesn't realise the wrong in their ways, the talk should have the essence of a debate with proper examples.

Parents should have this in their conscious mind throughout that their intention, however good for the child, needs a proper communication channel so that there is no drift in the relationship with their growing child. At each phase, the child will start feeling a drift even if the parents continue to communicate their intention in the same manner which had worked earlier.

It must be remembered that many things would affect a child once introduced to schooling. Peers play a significant role; a child feels like talking and being with friends, becoming essential in their lives. So, in cases where the peer group is seen to negatively affect a child, their peers must not be out-rightly dismissed or demeaned in front of the child. Again at this stage, there should be a rediscovery of communicating the intention. Such a manner should be adapted, which doesn't make the child feel that he has no outside source of knowledge except his parents. This would again cause a drift because each child wants to become an individual, and at tender ages, most of them wonder about fulfilling their whims which seem reasonable to them.

So, the scope to develop individually with flaws should be given to a child to self-learn. The child going through this phase of self-learning will sooner or later work out that parents who seemed to be strict actually did it for the best. To make the child self-realize there should be proper communication of their intentions until the child knows that they were right. Also, if this practice is successful, then the family can become more growing and developing in the future, where each one is heard for their opinions.

Imparting rather than imposing intentions of a practical nature will prove to be nothing less than a miracle. But this would require a perennial practice, which would have to be rediscovered and tailored for each stage in a child's life.

OF IDEOLOGIES: IN SEARCH OF THE ABSOLUTE

Perfection, accessibility, convenience, and being cordial are what the human race has sought after. There are various combinations in which order these four things have shaped human life. Out of these four things, one thing leads to another. Whatever is sought first has always led to the remaining three things in a particular order that forms the crux of an absolute or more articulated, Ideology.

Knowingly or Unknowingly, each individual makes their own ideologies. In the present era there is an overwhelming overlapping, most of the times unbeknownst to an individual. We think we seemingly own the merger going on globally because never has the world been more accessible to its diverse cultures and unique living styles.

Most of the thoughts and ideas we indulge in have already been practiced before. So there is now the thinnest line between personal ideology and a societal one.

Many of the individuals, sometimes unbeknownst to them, want an ideology that is perfect or absolute. So they don't adhere to the societal ideology, but such is the developed world today that there remains minute scope of improvising and forming one's own 'original' ideology.

It is imminent to notice here that each ideology, how much ever different, serves the purpose of being meaningful; leading a meaningful life. Forming a dogma, in reality, is the search for meaning, the absolute truth.

We can agree to the fact here that we all are imperfect unenlightened beings, and along with the clash of our ideologies, we have created considerable blunders in our world.

This is because most of our adopted ideologies have become our comfort zone, and it becomes one hell of a job to understand or even acknowledge another perspective. Unbeknownst to us, rigidity has perverted further development of our ideologies.

The perspective here plays a very intrinsic role in further maturing our ideologies. Person A can't over here gain perspective from Person B while Person A already abhors Person B's lifestyle or maybe even his way of clothing; yes, that's how the pest of rigidity has overpowered our actual development.

Most of us listen only to our loved ones, but only till a specific time. We do get saturated; although there still can be learning after the saturation point, we become ignorant due to the monotony of it all.

This leads us into a void that cannot be filled, and even the most influential attempts tend to fail.

So when a child comes into our lives, it becomes our second chance to reach a certain maturity level to see the bigger picture.

A child not imposed upon can teach the parents and themselves a more conducive ideology. For this, the child has to be given a free hand along with a counter-intuitive approach. These things are indispensable for the child in this era of constant changes.

Suppose the parent here tries to hammer their ideologies on the child already being beaten with many of them. In that case, the child will become confused, leading to various other complications later on. For the child, their parents are a massive influence in the initial years, so they will feel bound to discover things not discussed by the parent as they too want some meaning out of their lives.

A freehand doesn't mean spoiling your child but quenching the child's curiosity without patronizing so that later in life, the child doesn't keep mum about his queries and succumb to false or pseudo ideologies globally, such as terrorism.

It is the parent's duty to at least try to give reasonable logic to their child in an open-ended manner so that the child can start discerning their own reality. It will encourage the child to empower themselves with knowledge.

As they grow up with more than bookish knowledge, it will be those little experiences, that the parent at the time couldn't fathom would play a vital role, that will make them a wholesome individual.

The parents must not preach or impose as that will falter the whole process, and the child's absolute will become their parent's flawed ideology. The child must not feel he is not appropriately answered or ignored because that might stunt his emotional growth. Sometimes The child doesn't know how to react, so when an action is done by the child ensuring the parents that they were right about their child not understanding a particular thing must be overlooked and the parent must approach more gently in a different manner.

These instances will play a massive role in shaping the children, and even if it's not in their consciousness, they will definitely be the star performers in their subconscious.

The human race has not yet found out how the mind works, we are just moving forward with the complex manuals of the brain created by each others experiences, and thus there is a clash. So, we know that there is bound to be conflict or clashes of ideologies. Along with the development of their own ideology, the child should be nurtured in a manner wherein a clash or dispute can enable a new positive perspective in the child. This will be easier if the child develops a sharp sense of empathy.

Empathy can only be developed if the parents see their child as a teacher, not the authoritative one but the enlightened one. Noticing small things of their children will provide the parent with the clarity they didn't even know they were seeking. This clarity will empower them to nurture their child in a manner where the child learns empathy, and how to gain and act upon a new perspective because that is the prominent process of searching for the truth.

OF VALIDATION

Our world has developed, we have come to use various resources available in plenty. Some of the resources are exhausting, no doubt, but we have worked with them, utilized them in a scientific manner we have discovered. Thinking with clarity, we must realize that we have not yet gone to the next level in the most crucial resource we have, which helped govern the utilization of resources like wood, fossil fuels, metals, etc. That resource is our brain; of course, it has accustomed itself in a manner that promotes societal accessibility and convenience in a society.

But the point here is that we not only require physical but also emotional Validation. Why do people avoid crying in front of a group? They fear they will show their vulnerable side, which could later be manipulated, and in the same line of thought, they want to show their weaker sides. This is the main reason there are groups and even large communities who have gone through something similar. While a person without any diagnosis of mental illness won't get or even try to get a person's situation with it, the community formed will be massive support as the patient will find the respite of Validation.

In short, with the development of our world, it has also become quite diverse, and only the success stories coming out from each corner is strengthening the intricate fabric in our society. Still, people have not become more empathy-prone because this development has become a complex survival process for an individual's standard or satisfaction.

Such busy have our lives become that we seek Validation within our immediate reality, thereby making us more rigid to the diverse reality of other lives on our planet. Also, we have become dependent on such Validation as it makes us cozy in our comfort zones.

Even if an individual is flexible enough, he would want to seek Validation in the diverse spheres he indulges in. A minuscule number of people stay true to their own goals, their own reality, and most of them are satisfied with a pre-conceived validation that they have got and don't want to grow out of it even if problems are arising in this situation.

It is imminent to point out here that Validation has become an enormous hurdle and has stunted the growth of Humanity. Looking at the population, there is not even a double-digit number of people who have brought in something novel globally as each one of us has set our validation standards on the older things. They are no more valid or have become obsolete, but change is essential, especially when our society is shooting its branches in all directions; we need to adapt.

The majority of us have set our standards so that we don't realize that these are, in reality, the embodiment of someone long gone from this world. Of course, even this is not that much of a problem if we stay true to our standards. Which some of them do and find a reality true to it in every aspect.

In what we could call a paradox regarding the lack of novelty, there are now many new things, items, processes to indulge in. And, we indulge in them, mainly the consumption of information on a large scale on the internet. This indulgence increases our appetite for Validation in each sphere we have superficially touched; obviously, we are beings governed by our egos.

Now imagine a baby who has come into this world of confusion created by us adults. How can a baby survive and grow into a being which knows how to set its living standards and where they would need Validation?

There can be two approaches here, the first one being that we keep the child on one track and hope that this track merges into the flow of reality of the world and realizations are made by the child whilst forming their own truth.

The second one being a little opposite. The child is shown various perspectives upon a question asked and not just paint the answer in one color, and hopefully, this flow of reality through the child's mind then catches onto one wavelength that the child would like to call their own existence.

Both the approaches would work, but it has to be chosen with great care, looking at the child and what they are adept to. Of course, with the diverseness in the world, both approaches could be used for different things. Still, the parent has to remember that the importance of the chosen method has to be considerably more so that the child doesn't become confused in this Validation seeking world.

OF INHIBITIONS AND PROXIMITY

As a parent, one must know the meaning of two words: Inhibition and Proximity. Acknowledging their meanings and using them in their lives will prove to be very helpful and nourishing in their child's growth.

A child needs proximity from their parents, there is no substitute for that, but the society we live in there is an interaction of people on an everyday basis. As the child ages, a parent needs to know that his proximity to the world will increase. They should not have inhibitions about their child interacting with others, as an inhibition will only cause unnecessary restrictions that could even cause harmful situations or behavior against the parent's good intentions.

The other side of the coin here is that the child with such close proximity with new faces will develop its own set of inhibitions which the child will work through. Of course, the child being unused to such novel interactions and in the child's own discovering of the world, there will be some unnecessary inhibitions developed. The parents need not forewarn their child here about such inhibitions in any manner. The parent must work through these inhibitions of their child to ensure the initial fragile phase of innocent ideologies being formed in their children so that they become ready for the future.

On the contrary, it is not harmful to have inhibitions; for example, do not talk to strangers. The child doesn't really register why that is the case. But as the child grows up to be an individual, this inhibition of not talking to strangers has to be grown out of, for reasons we all know.

There can be various exercises which we can term as ice-breakers. Of course, the parent doesn't always want their child to continuously learn from a terrible experience that would form an inhibition about what led to the bad experience, making the child more caged in their thoughts and action.

An ice-breaker isn't restricted because the child is shown only the wrong side of something, for example, drugs.

In a hypothetical example, suppose a child is shown images of a destitute drug addict, his symptoms, his low standing in life, his dependence on drugs and rehabilitation centers, and such agitating things. But without showing them how the addict feels happy and blissful in a drugged state and how there are several successful personalities in the world indulging in it to party, the child is still not privy to the entire picture.

However small this colorful side to drug abuse is, the child should also be educated about it because the parent won't know what circumstances and situations will arise in their child's life. In those moments, the child must feel that he was not just shown one side of the story and that he knows the highs and lows of such a thing, enabling him to make a consciously rational decision. But suppose the child had been inhibited about drug use or even cigarettes for that matter, if a situation arises due to peer pressure to just take a drag of a cigarette, and the child obliges. In that case, he will enter into a realm he hadn't known before, the temporary high, and his inhibition will break easily as it has no natural base of deeper understanding.

Obviously, even a successful ice-breaker won't ensure that the child always takes the decision feasible for their well-being. Still, it will play a positively vital role when the child is faced with such decision-making situations. The ice-breakers will make an in-depth intricate base of understanding where the child will be in the realm of practicality rather than their whims, especially during their teens when they enter the kingdom of self-decision making.

If they acknowledge the proximity they have with someone and are free of inhibitions or understand the true nature of things they are in, then that will give them a free hand to change their course of development into a positive and beneficial one.

As a final note, inhibitions are not wrong, but they restrict us as we fear something which could turn out to be good for us. When something about which we have inhibitions is horrible for us, then an inhibition about the same can be self-deprecating because we fear that thing, and most of the time, what we fear, we don't understand or even try to. If we don't understand something that is affecting us, then it will stunt anyone's perceptive growth, be it a parent or their child.

To understand the above lines, we can take an example of a student who doesn't like maths as when they opened the book, they failed to get the answers correct to specific questions, so they start fearing it without putting in the efforts to understand it. This will prevent the student from sitting with the maths book and trying to understand those sums, thereby preventing them from the knowledge whether they could be adept at it or not. If the student continues with the inhibition without trying to understand and simply fearing the subject's lecture, homework, and eventually tests or exams, then unbeknownst to the student, there grows a void full of a lack of understanding. Whereas, with just a little more brave efforts, the student might have found the subject of maths as their forte and if not then at least a way to work around it. But the inhibition about maths simply restricts the students in that subject. Still, the student will find a habit formed where they choose to have inhibitions about various things in life, which will become their comfort zone. Once that gets broken somewhere down the line, it can be a difficult phase of life, and such stages evidently, in our world, have even led to suicides among students in large numbers.

The takeaway here is that we are bound to make decisions that will be detrimental to us. So in a child and even in parents, there should be an approach of understanding their fears so that even in the face of their deepest fears, they do not steer themselves into a fatal or destructive accident. Not all of us are trained or even ready to face adversity at any moment of our lives. Still, suppose we have a concrete foundation of the fundamental understandings in our lives. In that case, we will at least be in a position where we can altogether avoid or work around crises or adversities. This could only be done with closer proximity towards understanding which provides perspectives rather than generate cocoons of our inhibitions in the dark.

OF APPRECIATING LIFE

One has only so much time with themselves and their immediate reality in one life. Being a parent, in truth, means one has got a second chance to grow. Of course, not everyone can become flawless and perfect, but it is the journey towards it that matters. If one consciously starts this journey, there will be an appreciation and realization of the beauty of life; it will be an overwhelming and humbling experience. If one realizes that this journey could still be taken after having a child, there will be no need to worry about how to parent. The acknowledgment of flaws and moving distant from them along with growing with the child, listening to the child, recalling our bad experiences to the child if done in a healthy manner will be beneficial for the child's innocence and sense of wonder. In that case, one can outgrow the negatives in one's life, and even the child will not have to face the same negative situations as the parent.

There is no denying that in this diverse world of ours, even if a child is developed just perfectly, even then, there will be a set of problems. So, the approach should be not to pamper the child away from small or big problems but to make them capable of tackling such situations in a feasible and constructive manner.

True, no one is ever fully equipped with tackling each situation in life. Still, such should be the development of the child that they can use the pieces of equipment they have to make the situation feasible for themselves at the moment of a problem. This aptitude is not inherent and comes from proper nurturing and care directed towards making the child aware of their childhood. Only by being aware can one adapt to a particular situation, be it bad or good, because if one cannot gauze a problem, how will one know how to adapt to it? So, being aware is indispensable in this life.

A parent can only achieve this awareness in their child only when they are aware of the child's sense of wonderment and innocence and work accordingly, in a tailor-made fashion. There is always an inherent understanding in children towards a certain things and aspects of life; the parent must become aware of it and work with their child.

Sometimes as a parent we look at the antiques of our child and compare them with other children, thinking that when will the kid outgrow from their antiques. That is the point where awareness from the parents' side is needed to know that this is their child's unique nature, and as a parent, we will have to work with what we have. Like some vegetables cannot be grown in the mountains, mountain people grow certain vegetables suited to the altitude, soil, and other mountain factors. It will not be that easy for the parent to be aware of such things in their child. As the parents have come far from their innocence and sense of wonderment, that has become their reality. So most parents indirectly and directly want their children to outgrow their innocence and sense of wonder. But just imagine if we work along with the child's innocence. Because working with the simple, innocent ways of the child, the child will become more confident and more rooted in a manner because the parent is now working with what the child truly believes in.

Working with the child's innocence doesn't mean making the child whimsical. Instead, it means working with those whims in a manner to show the child how unfeasible, such things could be, so yes, a certain measure of control should be there, just so much, so that the child realizes and acknowledges the innocent ways the child is growing with and from. This will keep intact the child's innocence and measure how the world is different and similar to the child.

Suppose this measure in the child's mind is achieved. In that case, we won't need the child to follow monotonous rituals, like praying and thanking God before starting dinner (though quite a humbling practice), because the child will automatically come to appreciate things of their own accord. Suppose the child leads a life of enjoying everything that is there in a moment, the moments in which the child works towards a specific goal. In that case, even those moments won't feel bad as there will be an awareness of growth in him, which will bring in the appreciation, the child through various stages of life will know that they are content and are just working towards achieving self-growth.

When this seed of self-growth is imbibed in their cores, they will be successful in life. And, unlike so many others, be content and appreciative of their past and present. This is indispensable for their self-growth. Obviously, there will be failures, but the humbling concept of self-growth will only make them strive harder with an appreciation for themselves and their parents. Then there will come a time when they know the extent to which they can go, and at each step, they will outgrow their previous limitations.

The feeling of achievement that comes from outgrowing their previous limitations will be an essential factor towards their self-growth. Thus, they will be empowered in their own rights, in the sense that they will even appreciate those difficult moments or times they will go through.

So, the biggest takeaway here is that each child is different in their own unique ways. The parent has to wear a lens (metaphorically) and identify the innocence and sense of wonder in them, and instead of trying to make them outgrow it through strict and baseless rules, they should work with it. In short, a parent has to look through the lens that their child is wearing. Looking through your child's lenses try to see what the child sees and this knowledge will enable the parent as a nurturer and carer, and this empowerment will, in turn, result in the empowerment of their child. Because if the parent doesn't feel empowered with their child, then the child will sense that, and there will be a lot of confusion leading to uninvited problems which the child had not consciously asked for, and thus there will be no appreciation for life from the beginning.

Its important to understand your child as a parent, the child is a life we have conceived, and that doesn't mean the parent should impose on that life. There should be respect for the new life the parents have conceived and try to have a healthy curiosity about that life, enabling them to untangle themselves. Of course, respect for the new life means acknowledging that the energy is unique to their world and can take time to adapt, and the parent has to be practice patience and perseverance during the time that new life takes to adjust. Lastly, in familiarising with the world, the new life is scientifically proven to mimic and imitate, that's the reason, in this essay, there is a mention that a parent gets a second chance to grow, out of their flaws and expand their perceptions through their journey of lives together with their child.

OF INTENTION, QUESTION AND ACTION

The IQA approach towards parenting can especially be helpful with the child's development in the child's early years.

When the child adapts to a language and learns to speak in the initial years, a parent must not always talk to them in directional statements. It may stunt the child's reasoning power and development.

Of course, the parent's intention from the beginning with their child is to start understanding things. While there is no proper definition of understanding in a child's brain, they are not yet familiar with the quantitative quality we have recognized in our lives. At this stage, the child has no specific mark or, let's say, a concrete perspective which the child can consult while discovering new things.

So a perfect approach towards the child's reasoning development which will prove to be feasible in the child's later life could be to present questions to them. The questions can range from simple to complex once the child has started to try to speak. Yes, this approach has to be done during the onset of a child entering the realm of language. At their tender ages, the child has an intrinsic curiosity in them, so while posing a question, the parent need not worry whether the child has wholly understood it or not because there will be an internal process in the child to understand the question and try to answer them. This process in the child will make them familiarise themselves with the concept of understanding.

Most of us in our lives understand things but cannot act accordingly or even feasibly; we tend to get irrational towards our understanding, converting our intellect against ourselves as with some insights, we find ourselves in unfamiliar territory.

Asking your child questions, instead of directing them repeatedly or even punishing them for going against the directions, will build in them a more intricate fabric of reasoning. They will be able to be their own individuals later. For example, if a child is repeatedly doing something incorrectly and being reprimanded, they could become closed in thick shells, making them rebellious for no definite purpose. As simple as this situation sounds, a parent has to bear it and the child more so. Making the child learn by asking them questions about their behavior, their toys, their fears, their food habits, and so on will make them more independent and positively nurture them.

In the IQA approach, the intention comes before a question because the parent's intention must consist of only two things, i.e., make the child understand something in the child's own capacity and secondly, push forward the parent's understanding of their child. The basic premise here is that the question should serve no other manipulative purpose other than simply posing a query in which you want the child's perspective. If the questions become manipulative, then again, the child will not be able to become independent.

However, after posing a question with the intentions mentioned above, the next stage is to observe the child's actions and try to analyze the more minor things in their developing psyche. With keen observation, a parent will know their child and will be able to make tailor-made questions which could promote their child's development.

Of course, the child must be informed with the parent's perspective and, more than that, the world's, in such a manner, that the child is kept safe from generalizing or labeling. Because, at this stage, we are not trying to inject an ideology in the child but just understanding of things and a stark knowledge in them that an experience is vital towards moving forward.

If the IQA approach is taken, the parents also have to supplement them with more answers than the total number of questions, and at such times, parents tend to get impatient with the child. This will only make the child develop something negative as they want their daily doses of answers to process things, so a parent must not get demanding on the child by getting irritated by them. Remember, the child is a blank slate and is trying to garner as much information and understanding as possible.

But the child is carefree in those initial years, so this approach will also lead to more iterations of the same thing explained or asked as the child's brain is starting the process of imprinting and the child is primarily busy in the sense of wonder for new things encountered.

This approach will test a parent's patience, and the parent has to reinvent their limit, which would also prove helpful for the parent, and there will be the discovery of new perspectives not only for the child but also for the parent. So the parent and child must become conversant of each other, and this approach should not be followed blindly, but by observing the child's action and reaction, it has to be tailor-made.

The parent will discover that the child does not understand everything correctly; there must be a bifurcation regarding selecting things that need to be steered towards a specific direction. Not every tiny thing should be emphasized upon, remember the child has to start processing themselves too. So, prioritizing must be there when deciding which course to take with the child during a particular situation.

During the IQA approach, a parent might also discover that a child seems to understand the things simply iterated to them and follow them. But even if the questioning approach doesn't seem to help, the parent must remember that it is developing the child's psyche internally. After all, we don't want a child to become a sheep that follows others, but to have their own reasoning power, which will later help in life during demanding situations. So a parent must accept those repetitive, more minor mistakes and continue with the approach as its results will be better in the long term. So the current errors which are repeated will make the child learn with a certain depth about themselves and prevent them from causing more significant mistakes when they find themselves facing a situation alone.

The word 'action' has been used here because there will at least be a response in the child's psyche, if not verbally or in written form. The verbal response can be different from their mental response; for example, a child might be distressed, sad, or angry while sharing a toy with others, but the action of sharing a toy shows so many things. One of them is that the child has at least acted upon something and if there is an action, whether voluntarily or involuntarily, it becomes easier for the parents to know their child better. They can easily know their child's understanding and growth at various phases of their development. And a cordial discussion among the parents or guardians of the child will always lead to the most reasonable and feasible solution to the many situations during the child's nurturing.

OF KNOWLEDGE

There are some chapters in the life of a parent which they are afraid of. They don't know how to read their chapters or analyse them, they get stuck there. That chapter stays in the background affecting their lives.

Parents can solve this problem by sharing their chapters with their kids to become an individual. Parents don't do this, thinking they can control their children, but the parents need to get out of control of their lives' chapters to strive for rationality in their children. Of course, the child will soon develop his own rationale, but it would corrupt many things that needed no corruption. By disclosing chapters to your children, they can achieve a piece of their parents, which is what they want, need, and aspire to.

A child already has insurmountable love to give to their parents, but how could the child love them in darkness. For the child would just become dependent again in darkness, just like in the womb. The birthright of every child should be knowing, not simply right & wrong but simply knowing. The parents must ensure that.

If the judgment on the child starts at an early age, a forceful one, an imposing one, then the child will learn to judge and punish themselves. The child is entirely dependent on knowledge of a parent's chapters, the dark ones, the lighter ones, the in-between ones, for the child truly connects only with his parents. It is the parents who don't try to connect with the child sometimes, so the child pursues to be in accordance, but, in reality, it is their parents they want to connect with at every level possible. The stories of their parents can provide children with a ton of insight.

OF FEAR

We think knowledge is power. But an instinct can be more so at certain times. We are free to choose those times, but there comes a time that it is within a framework we are selecting and imparting.

If the child is seen to work outside of the framework created by the parents and parents cannot bring that framework in their knowledge or instincts, then talking it out with the child is of the utmost importance. Otherwise, this could cause the most futile, unnecessary, and most of all, debilitating clashes in the family.

There might be some inhibitions that are not in the child's mind yet. This is the time the parent can rediscover the child in them. Of course, this doesn't mean to try to play with fire. For example, If a parent who is scared of spiders notices their child to try to get hold of a spider and eat it then, the least a parent can do is not to instill the same fear of spiders in their child and inform their child about the life present in spider so that they don't hurt it. Also, the child could be informed about various facts and trivia about spiders at this time. If the parent is unaware then they should make the effort to surf the internet for information to share with their child. This again is an education that the child will learn to appreciate and also will look forward to. Further, this will not promote unreasonable fear of the parent in their children and they would realise that their parents are interested in informing them about new things and are truly concerned about them.

At some stage in their lives, every parent must have thought that they don't want to be like their parents. Mainly because they see through them and know what had gone wrong. A parent should choose to show their children their wrong choices so that they become informed and are not unreasonably fearful of dire situations. This self-awareness with the proper guidance can inculcate love and compassion in the child.

OF WORLD SCENARIO

These are the time of tumultuous jobs with low income and respect. A parent, mother, or father is bound to feel inferior. Domestic violence and abuse have become a part of most homes.

It has not been controlled effectively. There already lies a conflict between the mother and father in so many things that sometimes it could become very unhealthy for the child.

The usual scenario is to make the child live with the mother while the father works and earns. The less time a father spends with a child already takes a toll, even if the best places and things are provided for. A child is not a computer which needs new software to be updated, at least not in the easy fashion one installs a new update on their mobiles and computers these days.

Therefore, the decision for a child must be taken with a rigorous and holistic approach. Whether a couple is planning for a single child or multiple, they should ensure interchangeable responsibilities at the start.

After the child comes, a parent should ensure that they are everything to the child and that they shouldn't try to impose more minor things on them until they know their child's behavior. A second child shouldn't be planned just because their first one seems to be incorrigible. Also, the first or a single child shouldn't be neglected in the context of time. Time is essential, whatever the activity be. As the child grows, more time should be given to talking. Talk everything out with the child.

As the child grows, there will be influences where a parent won't know what has a bad or good effect on the child. In such scenarios, talking out could include some light-hearted discussion of 'taboo' topics so that when the child opens up, the good or bad influencers could be seen, and an understanding could be provided which could shape their child's understanding into a beneficial and constructive one.

OF FRIENDSHIP
AND RESPECT

Being a friend to a child is essential in so many aspects of parenting. But, it starts with the parents, the mother and the father becoming friends with each other.

Soon the parents realize that their child is influenced by how the parent duo is conversing with each other.

This is the time in marriage to start talking again when the child is not present. Conversing in a placating and authoritative manner, the couple needs to become each other's parents. If not entirely possible, they have to access their child's memories and then access their child's behavior after a, particularly nasty fight 'at home'.

The fight could have been because of the child, interpersonal parent relationship, or simply due to some minor or significant marriage or financial problems.

The child does realize the tension in the air. Parents don't need to be happy but talking in placating, and authoritative tones can help the child form an internal and external understanding.

There will be times when the fight is about the child; such disputes or discussions which could get heated should strictly not be done in front of the child until he comes of age. For their lies a deep need of love in the child, which gets filled with guilt; guilt, which the child doesn't know where to put in later life. So the tense turmoils of childhood, if not appropriately vented among the family members, can create unforeseeable problems for the child in the future.

There will obviously be moments when temper is lost, but that doesn't mean there should be repetitive apologies for the same, or the child will expect it every time. The apologies should be made with a holistic approach. For example, if the child is shouted at and reprimanded after a seemingly minor misdemeanor and one of the parents literally irrationally loses their temper, then the damage is done. The only thing a parent can do in this situation is not repeating the same charade again and work towards a holistic apology which would also involve not patronizing the child. Also, the other parent should handle it diplomatically so that the tempers on both the sides are satiated in a manner which promotes understanding between each other. Such instances should be given significant talking out times to know where else the child is feeling suffocated with their parenting.

If Parents lose temper in their personal fight or because of the child, then it is of utmost importance to be respectful to each other as a parent. For this is the time, the couple is looking at their partners in a new light. Even a ten-minute understanding conversation could help in sorting out their fight. Such discussions can turn parenting from controlling to a more holistic and nourishing attitude.

So apart from being a friend to their children parents need to treat each other with respect too, this will set an empowering example for their child.

OF POWER AND INDULGENCE

As an adult, we all can boast to ourselves of undergoing and successfully tackling various phases of our life. We become experienced, and thus a parent is better suited to gauge the potential of their children. But, an important thing to note here is that the parent estimates the child's potential according to their set frequency. Seldom do parents go out of their own drawn line and look beyond their inner norms and rituals. After all the noise a youth has made about making a difference, we all come to a stage where we fear something different and out of our routine lives. We think the cocoon we have woven for ourselves is the perfect one and thereby start the process of judging and labeling because that is the only way we know to guard our precious way of life.

A child, however, is an entirely new life and has infinite number of possibilities. Being at the same frequency a parent operates at, one can go astray. Knowingly or unknowingly, a parent tries to attune their children to their frequency. They only see the empty part of them that needs to be filled, ignoring the life that is gushing in and out of their children. Discipline is indeed healthy for children, but a parent sometimes tends to forget the level child is starting from, during its implementation. We try to include so many things in discipline, mostly our failures. If one form of loss is prevented, the child is bound to fail in other things. The discipline should serve it purpose of imparting and instilling knowledge rather than setting a strict unreasonable regime that becomes toxic and hampers a productive growth of their child.

Living our lives, we tend to forget the basic part and parcels of life for our children. Parents think everything could be prevented and made foolproof for our children if they only follow their parents. Parents ignore the immense diversity of life and ideologies which could be suited to their children. Finally, when the child has no breathing space after attuning to an ill-formed, useless frequency at which the parent is operating, they tend to have the first negative experiences in their early life which the parent has so blatantly tried to prevent.

Of course, as an experienced adult, a parent has the right to show and exercise their power over their children. But only to the extent where the path paved by a parent could then be simultaneously paved by their children until the children are ready to cross the tracks in their lives with other lives. The power should be exercised to generate energy rather than curb it. Curbing the child's ability at a base level can backfire at so many levels. It would then become a habit for the parent to spend long hours blaming themselves or others until a definite problem is pinpointed, and even that will not lead to a solution.

In each phase of children's growth, the child will need to exert and spend specific energies in a particular manner that will give them their own perspective and, thereby, a holistic growth. Being a strict disciplinarian and authoritarian around a child's thinking without any fruitful perceptions will only make the child dependant without any breathing space to grow themselves. However, it would be highly feasible for the child's perception and healthy growth where the parent understand and imbibes in themselves their role as nurturers, and carers that need to nourish their child with growth rather than becoming dictatorial masters of their child's lives which gives their child no perspective other than feeling closeted.

It is in the children's best interest where learning and discipline are not taught but are indulged into, by the parent's active participation. This active participation and indulgence can only be achieved when the parent stops checking their children at every level and starts checking themselves, especially when the children have become of a perceptive age.

A strict regime without any bends will only make the child less imaginative and perception-less bound to fall as soon as this make-believe regime changes, even a bit. A child needs to be flexible so that the various phases of life could be experienced as a fresh breeze of positive experiences, rather than trying to ace everything that comes their way without learning or perceiving anything out of life's significant experiences.

Indulging in a child's stupidity, and active involvement in their carefree times apart from just learning will give them breathing space and individual character. This is where the process of being self-made and standing on their own toes shall start at. A chance to being themselves and making them indulge and involve in things at their own level will provide them with the satisfaction of learning things at their own pace. This will enable a healthy and holistic internal and external growth in the child.

The powerful disciplinarian and authoritarian side can prevent the mistakes a parent has made, however, an indulgent and involved parent will learn new things that will invoke a child's simultaneous growth along with the parent's too. And, of course, they won't be stuck in a set inane disciplinarian loop which they would become dependent upon for their growth.

Of course, a healthy discipline is required. But not as a pretext and at the cost of parents behaving irresponsibly. Parents tend to overdo the disciplinary actions without knowing their child's unique requirements. Each child has their own set of difficulties that they need to overcome, and the parent must pass that power to them.

OF CONSTRUCTING 2+2

We generate our own equations to perceive our life realities in the process of our learning. The bond that a parent shares with their children is entirely based on the process of learning. Learning from children and making them understand is the basis of the bond created during our lifespan.

To generate a practical and solvable reality for the child, the child must know the variables and constants they will work with. First, the child must learn and get it into the system that not every $2+2 = 4$. It will do the child well if interpretations and perceptions are juggled healthily at an early age itself.

For this to happen smoothly, a child must be treated with utmost honesty without fearing their loss of 'innocence' by their parents. As many things the child could be introduced to during his early questioning phase, the better it will be for their mentally holistic growth. Not everything needs to be crammed up into the child, but each answer should be elaborate to the extent of the child's curiosity so that it reaches the almost blank core of the child and is imbibed by them.

Healthy talks, discussions, and debates should be started at an early age. Even if the child doesn't do well in these debates or discussions, the child and the parent will realize the field of aptitudes and ineptitude. This will help attune the child's frequency of learning to a level that will be helpful to the child at later stages. At an early age, all the things a child is grasping are at a minuscule level that will take time to germinate and blossom as everything seems to be happening at the back - end. So, patience and understanding on their parent's part is a must.

A child should be interacted with at a level that is the most feasible one for an individual stature. Learning should be introduced in a manner that seems like equipping the child with the necessities. If the child is adequately prepared, then a parent can breathe freely as to the level of the child's perception. Of course, not everything will be interpreted in a manner that will adhere to a parent's viewpoint. This will be the moment when the child will openly share the lens he is looking from. It can be shaped gently for the child's benefit. Still, if the parent tries to snatch away the lens without giving a better pair of the lens with admonishment and stating it wrong without adequate reasoning will hamper the child's perceptions and their subsequent development.

The next opportunity will come with great difficulty and wariness from the child's side. So it is essential to equip the child with knowledge but not to the extent that he cannot personalize it. The freedom of personalization is a must for a distinct and formidable identity of the child in his own mind. This shall prepare the child to live with dignity in a society.

An easy way to start this equipping is by setting examples as a parent and verbal reasoning with the child about what is acceptable in a society. Simply stating the norms and implying that they need to be followed blindly will only lead the child to look for a breathing space, and that particular breathing space could be poisonous and ultimately harmful or dangerous in nature. Although, if the child is treated in a manner wherein they have their own identity and their intellect, however, small it may seem at the time, is recognized then that will boost the child's internal and external confidence and inculcate a responsible conscience in the child's psyche. This will automatically push the child towards positive values in their life. Thereby, each positive value will make the child more optimistic in their interpretations, allowing a space where they could live and breathe freely to promote their healthy self-growth.

So, a child doesn't need to talk about the interpretations of life. Instead, he should be gently pushed towards making his own and shaping them with gentle discussions poking at the child's intellect and curiosity.

www.ingramcontent.com/pod-product-compliance
Lightning Source LLC
Chambersburg PA
CBHW061517250726
48657CB00005B/1927